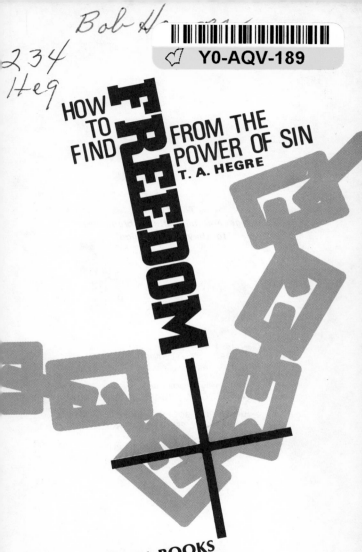

Bob H.

234
Heg

HOW TO FIND **FREEDOM** FROM THE POWER OF SIN

T. A. HEGRE

DIMENSION BOOKS
Bethany Fellowship, Inc.
Minneapolis, Minnesota

Y0-AQV-189

*To all who
"hunger and thirst after righteousness:
for they shall be filled"*

Originally published under the title:
THE WILL OF GOD...YOUR SANCTIFICATION

DIMENSION BOOKS are published by
BETHANY FELLOWSHIP, INC.
6820 Auto Club Road
Minneapolis, Minnesota 55431

Printed in the United States of America

CONTENTS

FOREWORD

Early in my spiritual life I was convinced both by Christian nurture and personal study of the Word of God that there is an experience for Christians in which they will find freedom from the power of sin. Finally this experience as embodied in the truth of sanctification by the Father, Son, and Holy Spirit became more than a theory and one of personal reality. But then I faced the problem of communicating the truth of such an experience to others so that they too would clearly understand what was meant by and what could and should be experientially sought for freedom from the power of sin in the Christian life.

All too often one has been impressed with the garbled message on sanctification even by some who are the most active proponents of God's sanctifying grace operating both in crisis and process in this life. Too often the word concepts are of men and not in the pattern of "Thus saith the Lord." Then again the theological interpretation of sanctification which may be so clear to the scholar is all too foggy to the man in the pew—and, one suspects, to the preacher in the pulpit who wants to communicate to the heart need of the man in the pew daily wrestling in his Christian walk with the power of sin.

As a result of my own desire to articulate God's truth clearly in this area I have read many books on the will of God in sanctification. Some have been mediocre, some good, and a few very good. But only a limited number have merited the accolade of 'excellent.' In my mind among the best of them all is this volume by an esteemed brother in the faith, T. A. Hegre of the Bethany Fellowship. I have been commending this work in the previous edition to fellow pastors, lay workers and seekers after truth in many denominations and fellowships.

I believe that the path is clearly enunciated herein on how to find deliverance from the power of sin in God's sanctifying grace. The Pauline phrase in Thessalonians, "The will of God, your sanctification," is soundly exegeted. This volume is excellent for the pastor's study with his membership classes, for collateral or textual reading for seminaries and colleges, and for the personal search of the honest seeker for God's sanctifying grace in his life. May this volume be blessed as an aid for those who press on in the path of that "holiness without which no man shall see the Lord."

Arthur M. Climenhaga, S.T.D., LL.D.
Bishop, Midwest-Pacific Conferences
Brethren in Christ Church

A PERSONAL NOTE

In the history of the Church, such Scriptural phrases as "holy in all manner of living," "sanctify you wholly," "free from sin," "perfect as your heavenly Father is perfect," have suffered much abuse and many wounds. In the religious world, many seem inclined to fear the doctrine and possibility of holiness in Christian experience more than the remains of uncleanness and bondage in the lives of Christians.

This book declares in a fresh and vital way that great truth of sanctification by the Father, the Son, and the Holy Spirit, not only as a wonderful prospect to be sought but also as an available blessing to be received and enjoyed.

It has been a very real benefit and enjoyment for me to work together with Ted Hegre in the ministry of both Bethany Church and of the Bethany Fellowship Missionary Training Center. As his assistant, I have come to understand and appreciate the very practical and even apostolic nature of the ministry the Lord Jesus has given him—a ministry that does not treat truth in a theoretical manner but rather as a practical issue, which in the person of Christ produces holiness and power.

This outworking has been proved right here in the

lives of ordinary men and women, many of whom are now scattered throughout the earth as witnesses for Christ.

The contents of this book have also been proclaimed by the author farther afield—in the homeland and across the sea. Wherever they have been proclaimed, deep spiritual transactions have been made. Here in our own church meetings and conferences, it has been a holy experience to minister (or be ministered unto) in an inquiry room among spiritually hungry men and women seeking the blessing described in this book. One soon realizes that in this message of deliverance, something more than the theories and persuasions of men are involved; in Christ's redemption, the very "powers of the age to come" are concentrated on making God's people pure and holy. God's sanctifying grace is real. May it be real to all who read these pages.

Harold J. Brokke
Assistant Principal
Bethany Fellowship
Missionary Training Center

PREFACE

Early in my Christian life I became aware of my own need of finding freedom from the power of sin. Though genuinely converted, and assured by the Holy Spirit of forgiveness of sins and eternal life, I was just as definitely assured that I needed something more besides daily growth. The high level of Christian walk outlined in the Bible was not my experience. In seeking help from books, I found that many writers wanted to convince me that my Christian life to date, as I had experienced it, was all that could be hoped for in this life. However, the Bible and my own longing contradicted this prospect. It was at this time that I began to seek the Lord in earnest. My deep hunger led me to an intense study of the Word of God. Here I found the answer to my own heart's cry in the Bible doctrine of sanctification.

I had already discovered that a great number of people were not aware that sustained victory is possible. Others, though long convinced by the Scriptures of its possibility, did not know how to appropriate God's provision. These needed to ask, as the Ethiopian asked Phillip, "How can I (understand) except some man shall guide me?" But I found no one to guide me, though many, had I only known of them, could well have done so. Nor, at that time, did I find books to help, except a Bible concordance which listed sanctification by the Father, Son and Holy Spirit, and a small tract by W. C. Stevens which did the same. Later, however, I found many books on this subject.

And so I began to pray and search the Scriptures for myself. This, in turn, led to experiencing both deliverance from the power of sin and also the infilling and anointing with the Holy Spirit. My experience was prolonged into three stages largely, perhaps, because of my lack of knowledge. First, I found a partial answer by making a full consecration to God; later, I discovered the recovering power of the blood and the delivering power of the Cross; still later, I learned the power of the Holy Spirit, who not only "indwells" but "infills" and "comes upon" to do His work both within and without the believer. Some time afterwards I saw that these three "stages" were really related to the three Persons in the Trinity, and that each Person had performed a very definite work in my experience. I knew that my experience would not have had to be drawn out over the years. It could have been entered into at one time; but my lack of light had delayed the full realization.

Aware of all this, and of the fact that many others were searching as once I had, I began to give messages showing sanctification through the Father, the Son, and the Holy Spirit—first in my own church, and then in other churches in the United States, and finally in many foreign countries. Because I found it easier to understand as well as accept this truth through a three-stage revelation and application, I have presented them in this fashion. I have now been prevailed upon to publish these truths in book form. Some of these chapters have already appeared in the magazine, The *Message of the Cross*. The chapter beginnings may therefore have more review and be more repetitious than is ordinarily warranted, but it has seemed good to leave a certain amount of repetition for better clarification and understanding of the message. This book is sent out with the hope that others will find the truth and reality of freedom from the power of sin, as well as the available power of God for living a holy and fruitful Christian life. No originality nor excellence in presentation is claimed—only the desire that others may enter into this blessed life.

T. A. H.

CHAPTER ONE

WHAT IS SANCTIFICATION?

WE have often been asked the following vital questions: "What is sanctification?" "What is the baptism with the Holy Spirit?" "Are these two experiences one and the same?" "Is one sanctified and filled with the Spirit when he is saved?" "Is sanctification progressive?" "Is one sanctified subsequent to regeneration, and then baptized with the Spirit subsequent to sanctification?" "Are all Christian experiences ours the moment we are regenerated, and is our part just to appropriate them as we have light and grace to do so?"

Before seeking the answer to these questions, we should first of all read two passages of Scripture:

"This is *the will of God*, even *your sanctification*" (I Thess. 4:3). "The grace of God hath appeared, bringing salvation to all men, instructing us, to the intent that, denying ungodliness and worldly lusts, we should live soberly and righteously and godly in this present world; looking for the blessed hope and appearing of the glory of the great God and our Saviour Jesus

Christ; who gave himself for us, that he might redeem us from *all* iniquity, and *purify unto himself a people for his own possession,* zealous of good works. These things speak and exhort and reprove with all authority. Let no man despise thee" (Titus 2:11–15).

These two passages are indeed a plain statement of what God expects of a Christian, and they are certainly very inclusive. Salvation, according to the Scriptures, means more than "a decision." The Apostle Paul speaks not only of *life* but of a *holy* life; and again he is not satisfied with a holy *life* but insists also on *service—holy* service.

We have heard the expression, "We don't want doctrine; we want life." Now at first this saying sounds very spiritual, but in reality it is nothing but a pious phrase. We do want doctrine; we want the teachings of the Bible and of the Spirit, set forth in the simplest terms. We want and need to know the truth. Jesus said, "Ye shall know the truth, and the truth shall make you free."

Then too, others say, "We don't want the blessing; we want the Blesser." Again we reject this statement and say rather that we want both the blessing and the Blesser; we want Christ *and* the genuine blessing, the blessing that will abide.

We are certainly right in asking the question, "What is sanctification?" We *must* know the answer, for God's Word says that sanctification is His will for us. In the broad sense, sanctification includes all Christian experience from justification to glorification, beginning with the new birth and continuing in the Christian life until we meet the Lord face to face. However, the word *sanctification* is also used in a narrower sense, referring to *a crisis experience following justification and regeneration.* (Justification is the legal aspect and regeneration the moral and vital aspect of our salvation. At salvation we are both forgiven and born again.) Yet salvation is just the beginning of the Christian life. After this experience we should grow in grace.

Even with a genuine experience of supernatural regeneration, one discovers that there is something within that retards growth. This "thing" is known by different names such as indwelling sin, the "old man," carnality, sinfulness, etc. The best term, however, is found in Isaiah 53:6, "All we like sheep have gone astray; we have turned every one to *his own way.*" Scriptural definitions eliminate many problems, and the Scriptural definition of this hindrance to growth is, as we have seen, "his own way" (sometimes referred to as "own-way-ness," selfishness, selfness, or the self-life).

In justification, all past sins are forgiven. If a sin should occur after the experience of justification, it too can be confessed and forgiven. But this own-way-ness, this selfness, this self-life can *not* be forgiven. It is a principle, a disposition to have one's own way, and therefore must end. Selfish acts *can* be forgiven, but basic selfishness has to end in crucifixion with Christ. The *blood* is God's remedy for sins; the *Cross* is God's remedy for the self-life. At the moment of salvation one is not too much concerned about the self-life, nor does one understand fully his own complex nature. He is mainly occupied with sin and the Saviour. It was so with Israel, who was delivered from Egypt in crossing the Red Sea (generally considered a type of salvation). But at Sinai, though very confident of her ability to obey God in everything, Israel miserably failed Him, experiencing that which we call self-discovery. In other words, she discovered the corruption of her self-life.

We today also need this deeper conviction, this self-discovery, this self-exposure. We must acknowledge, confess, repent of, and renounce all ungodly and worldly lusts (desires). Jesus Christ laid the axe right at the root of our problem when He said, "If any man would come after me, let him *deny himself*, and take up his cross, and follow me" (Matt. 16:24). This verse speaks of more than forgiveness. Here Christ gives the remedy for own-way-ness or the self-life. The answer is the Cross. As we have just said, the blood of Christ solves the sin problem; the Cross of Christ solves the self problem.

Colonel Brengle tells of a girl who came to him with the question, "What is this sanctification that people are talking so much about?" For nearly a year she had so heard the experience testified to, and

15

talked and preached about, that Colonel Brengle thought she understood the subject. Her question therefore surprised and almost discouraged him. But then he asked, "Have you a bad temper?"

"Oh yes," said she, "I have a temper like a volcano."

"Sanctification," he replied, "is to have that bad temper taken out." That definition set her thinking. It did her good. But it was too narrow, and Brengle therefore added, "If I had said, 'Sanctification is to have the temper *and all sin* taken away, as well as the heart filled with love to God and man,' it would have been a better definition of sanctification." Expression of anger in bad temper can be forgiven; something more, however, is needed to bring an end to the condition which caused this sin of anger. In order that the new life in Christ may have full expression in us, the salvation Christ provides delivers the soul from the *power* as well as the *guilt* of sin.

It has been said that the Christian's "new life" is God's life, only in a smaller measure. We quote: "A spark of fire is *like* fire. And again, the tiniest twig on the giant oak or the smallest branch on the vine has the nature of the oak or the vine. In this respect a branch is like the oak or the vine. Similarly, a drop of water from the ocean on the end of your finger is like the ocean—not in its size, of course (big ships cannot float upon it nor the big fishes swim in it), but it is like the ocean in its essence, its character, its nature. Just so, a sanctified person is *like* God—not that he is as infinite as God (he does not know everything; he has not all power and wisdom as God has), but he is like God in his nature . . . ; he is good, pure, loving, and just, in the same way that God is." The Bible says that he is a "partaker of the divine nature" (II Pet. 1:4). God's provision for constant victory is complete, but of course victory is dependent on our yieldedness and faith. A sanctified person, therefore, is like Jesus Christ, who was wholly given up to doing the Father's will, for He said, "I do always the things that are pleasing to him" (John 8:29).

As we said before, after the experience of supernatural regeneration, it would be normal and natural for a Christian to grow constantly if it were not for "that thing" which retards growth. Therefore, besides forgiveness, one must be cleansed from all sin. One's own-way-ness, spoken of by Isaiah, must be crucified. Self must be dethroned and committed to the Cross, and Christ must be enthroned. Moreover, a Christian *must be filled* with the Holy Spirit for an inner life of victory, and *must be clothed* with the Holy Spirit for power for service.

Sanctification, therefore, when we think of it in the narrower sense, has two sides: the negative and the positive. The negative side of our sanctification is that deep inner work of the blood and the Cross which cleanses and delivers from the power of sin; it is the cleansing from sin and the crucifixion of the self-life. The positive side of our sanctification is the baptism with the Holy Spirit when one is both filled with

17

the Holy Spirit and clothed with power from on high. Instead of the works of the flesh will be substituted the fruit of the Spirit—"love, joy, peace, longsuffering, kindness, goodness, faithfulness, meekness, self-control; against such there is no law" (Gal. 5:22, 23). The result of the positive side of our sanctification is power for holy, victorious living and for fruitful service. "John truly baptized with water; but ye shall be *baptized with the Holy Ghost* not many days hence. . . . But ye shall *receive power*, after that the Holy Ghost is come upon you: and ye shall *be witnesses* unto me both in Jerusalem, and in all Judæa, and in Samaria, and unto the uttermost part of the earth" (Acts 1:5, 8, A.V.).

CHAPTER TWO

SANCTIFICATION THROUGH GOD THE FATHER

IN Chapter 1 we stated that in the broad sense sanctification includes the entire Christian experience from regeneration to glorification. However, the word *sanctification* is also used in a narrower sense to describe a crisis experience of heart-cleansing—that is, the dethronement of self, the enthronement of Christ, and the baptism and filling with the Holy Spirit.

The experience of sanctification is so tremendously important both to God and to us that each person of the Trinity is vitally concerned and has an official and distinctly personal part to perform in the realization of this work of grace in our lives. For that reason it is important to understand and cooperate with the work and blessing of the Father, Son, and Holy Spirit.

The word sanctification is often defined in a threefold way: (1) "to dedicate"; (2) "to set aside for holy uses"; (3) "to make holy." All of this is God's perfect plan and provision for a life of inner victory and power for service. This triple character of our

19

sanctification—each person of the Trinity performing a specific and definite work in this, God's great recovery program—explains why certain believers are called sanctified in Scripture while at the same time they give evidence that there is something lacking in their experience. For instance, in the first chapter of First Corinthians, the believers in Corinth are spoken of as sanctified; yet in the third chapter, the Apostle Paul calls them carnal. That they are genuinely converted is evident, for he designates them as "babes in Christ" (3:1). Therefore they were sanctified in the sense of being "dedicated to God," "set aside for holy uses." Righteousness had been imputed but not yet imparted. They had not yet been "made holy." They had a positional holiness, but it had not yet become practical in their everyday life and walk. They were not entirely sanctified.

The fact that sanctification is ascribed to each of the three persons of the Trinity is seen from the following verses of Scripture.

Sanctified through God the Father

"Jude, the servant of Jesus Christ, and brother of James, to them that are sanctified by God the Father . . ." (Jude 1, A.V.).

"The God of peace himself sanctify you wholly; and may your spirit and soul and body be preserved entire, without blame at the coming of our Lord Jesus Christ" (I Thess. 5:23).

20

Sanctified through God the Son

"Jesus also, that he might sanctify the people through his own blood, suffered without the gate" (Heb. 13:12).

"By one offering he hath perfected forever them that are sanctified" (Heb. 10:14).

"Christ also loved the church, and gave himself up for it; that he might sanctify it, having cleansed it by the washing of water with the word, that he might present the church to himself a glorious church, not having spot or wrinkle or any such thing; but that it should be holy and without blemish" (Eph. 5:25–27).

Sanctified through God the Holy Spirit

"According to the foreknowledge of God the Father, in sanctification of the Spirit . . ." (I Pet. 1:2).

"But ye were washed, but ye were sanctified, but ye were justified in the name of the Lord Jesus Christ, and in the Spirit of our God" (I Cor. 6:11).

"We are bound to give thanks to God always for you, brethren beloved of the Lord, for that God chose you from the beginning unto salvation in sanctification of the Spirit and belief of the truth" (II Thess. 2:13).

"...that the offering up of the Gentiles might be made acceptable, being sanctified by the Holy Spirit" (Rom. 15:16).

Our study is first to find out the specific work in our sanctification which each person of the Trinity performs and then to learn how to cooperate, that is, how to receive the blessing that is offered. We shall begin with "sanctified by God the Father. . ." (Jude 1:1, A.V.). What distinctive work does our heavenly Father perform in our sanctification? First of all, we see in I Thessalonians 4:3 that He calls us to this wonderful experience: "This is the will of God, even your sanctification." We know, therefore, it is His will, His desire, that we be sanctified.

In Ephesians 2:10 we read that God has a definite plan for every one of us: "We are his workmanship, created in Christ Jesus for good works, which God afore prepared that we should walk in them." We must be willing not only to accept that plan, but we must "enter into it" by faith. This is consecration. In Proverbs 23:26 God says, "My son, give me thy heart." Here He is not talking to the unregenerate (He never calls one not born from above "My son"). He is talking to one who has been genuinely born of God. He is talking to a son, and He is saying that He wants the entire heart of every child of His. According to these two verses, then, God the Father is calling us to sanctification, to full surrender, and to full consecration—to a wholehearted "yes" to our heavenly Father's will in every particular.

However, in our conversion experience we are not very conscious of the need of sanctification. It is *after* conversion, *after* genuine justification and regeneration, that we begin to realize the true meaning of the claims of God. A child of God soon discovers also that he is not wholly surrendered, that he is not wholly consecrated. We ought to bear in mind concerning the words *surrender* and *consecration* that strictly speaking there is a distinction in the meaning of these two words. Surrender is giving up; it is yielding; it is waving a white flag. But consecration is more than that. Consecration is not only yielding wholly to God in the sense of giving up going one's own way, but it is also gladly embracing the whole will of God. In army terms, consecration would mean not only waving the white flag and ending the battle, but would also include gladly changing sides and living and fighting for the conqueror. Consecration is really the highest type of surrender.

In his conversion experience, the believer already made adjustments to all known sin and to all the known will of God. Later, however, he received more light and discovered that he must take another step— complete consecration, even of possessions, privileges, position, ambitions, attitudes, opinions, persons, pleasures, places, of absolutely everything, including his own will in its entirety.

Can we know that we are fully consecrated to God? Yes, not only *can* we know but we *must* know. If we do not know that we are wholly yielded to

God, it is a sign we have not wholly surrendered. We often hear it said, "I am surrendered as far as I know." That statement is a dead giveaway. When we are wholly surrendered and wholly consecrated to God, we know it. The heavenly Father not only calls us to such a total consecration, but when it is complete, He receives us to himself in a new way and gives us the assurance that the issue is now a settled matter. Of course He cannot witness to this experience before it takes place; therefore, many today may be genuinely converted but they have no assurance of being wholly yielded to God. They have never heard the sweet witness of God's assurance that their surrender is accepted, that their consecration is complete.

In the eighteenth chapter of Jeremiah's prophecy, there is an illustration of a potter and the clay. Jeremiah says,

> "I went down to the potter's house, and, behold, he was making a work on the wheels. And when the vessel that he made of the clay was *marred* in the hand of the potter, he *made it again* another vessel, as it seemed good to the potter to make it."

Apparently Jeremiah's potter had no difficulty at all in the initial forming of a vessel according to his own plan. Even when the vessel had to be remade, the potter had no difficulty, for in clay there is no opposing will. It may sometimes be too soft or too hard to work; or sometimes it may even contain a hidden stone. But an earthly potter knows just what to do, and is never hindered—either in his original or remedial plan.

In human experience these same conditions of softness and hardness are common, so the heavenly Potter continues to work with the clay. Yet, if the will is not yielded, it is impossible for Him to make this human clay "meet for the Master's use." Once the will is yielded, then He is able to remove hidden stones of secret sin and, through batting and kneading, get human clay to the right consistency. If there is nothing to hinder, He can make us exactly what He wants us to be.

Consecration to God, then, is not to be passive. It is not enough just to surrender. We must actively exercise faith, and in obedience to God's wonderful Word, cooperate with our heavenly Father. We must also believe He receives the surrender. Then God is able to make, and mold, and conform us to the image of Jesus Christ.

Here, then, is the first step in sanctification—full consecration to the heavenly Father's will—so complete a consecration that God can witness to it, and we ourselves can receive wonderful assurance that we are wholly His in a new way. Andrew Murray said, "God is ready to assume full responsibility for the life wholly yielded to Him." This is the beginning work of our sanctification. Remember, God *wants* us to be entirely sanctified. The important thing to see is that in this part of our sanctification it is not only the Father's calling us to full consecration, but His receiving our consecration and giving us assurance that this wonderful possibility has become a reality.

Perhaps a personal testimony will help someone to understand this aspect of our subject—the beginnings of sanctification. After the writer's conversion at the age of twenty or twenty-one, he was an earnest Christian. He took very seriously his new relationship to God and his new responsibility as a child of God; consequently he became a member of most boards and organizations of his church. Because he was very serious and sincere, he was able outwardly to live an exemplary Christian life. However, he himself knew that everything was not well inside. He knew that though he had peace with God through Christ, and though he had assurance of salvation, he did not always have harmony in his heart. Many times there was a conflict within. Romans 7 perhaps would be the best description of his condition: "Not what I would, that do I practise; but what I hate, that I do" (vs. 15).

One night at a church prayer meeting, two choruses were sung—one, "Every day with Jesus is sweeter than the day before"; and the other, "I am satisfied with Jesus." The writer started singing, but because his heart was honest, he had to cease, for these statements simply were not true in his own experience. It would not be right, he thought, to sing or to say what was a lie. Then he seemed to remember that often at prayer meetings, testimonies were given; so he thought to himself, "Well, I'll give a testimony, but I'll tell the truth. I will testify to my salvation, but will confess, too, that I do *not* have perfect peace and harmony in my soul. Usually I have obeyed God eventually, but often there has been an argument with Him first. I have made proper adjustments from time to time, but even so, there still has been conflict within—sometimes more, sometimes less. Even now, at the proper provocation conflict can and does arise. I have self-control and restraint enough to conceal this, but it is there nevertheless. The whole outward life is regulated, but the inner life is not." But then after thinking about testifying, the writer decided not to give his inner thoughts in testimony, lest he upset some whom he had influenced for the Lord.

After prayer meeting he went to the man whom he considered the most spiritual in the church, told him his inner thoughts about singing the two choruses, and ended by saying, "Jesus is *not* sweeter than the day before, for He was sweeter to me two or three years ago than He is now. I just am *not* satisfied with Jesus, and I know He is not satisfied with me. What shall I do?" This dear Christian hung his head for a moment, and then said, "I don't know what you should do. I'm not satisfied myself." Utterly disappointed, the writer left his friend and went home. He was alone in the house and so went right to the Lord and prayed something like this: "I am not satisfied. There must be more to the Christian life than I have. God, You are holding out on me. You *must* reveal to me what I need. Must man wait for the grave to deliver?"

Then it seemed the Lord led him to read a book entitled *Absolute Surrender* by Andrew Murray. (Somehow he knew his problem was on the line of surrender.) He read on until he came to the place where Mr. Murray made a suggestion something like this: "Get down on your knees before God and surrender all you are and have and ever will have—*and your own will besides.*" The writer knew this was not the whole answer, for he had already tried to make such a surrender several times. At best it had lasted only a few days or at the most a week or so. Therefore he argued both with God and with Andrew Murray (though Andrew Murray, as you know, had long since left this earth for a better place). Then he read on and saw in the lines something like this: "*Get up from your knees believing God has received your surrender.*" Here was something new. Here was something he had never seen before. Here was the other side of the surrender experience. He had often heard ministers and others encouraging people to surrender wholly to God; but never had he heard anyone give this other side—namely, when one surrenders, God receives; and if God receives, He will assume full responsibility for the life.

And so, that very night the writer yielded wholly to God, believed God received his surrender, and then jumped to his feet and praised the Lord for the deliverance and the assurance that had come into his heart. For six months he almost walked on air. He knew God had done a real work of grace in his heart—giving peace, harmony, rest, wonderful answers to prayer, and blessings in many ways. Later on he discovered other needs, which will be discussed in the next chapters.

CHAPTER THREE

SANCTIFICATION THROUGH GOD THE SON

WE stated already that the experience of sanctification is so tremendously important both to God and to us that each person of the Trinity is vitally concerned and occupied in performing this work of grace. Moreover, the word sanctify has a three-fold meaning: to dedicate; to set aside for holy use; to make holy. If we keep in mind the fact that different Scripture passages give us different aspects of sanctification, and all passages must be considered and harmonized to give us a clear and complete meaning, we will have no problem concerning the meaning of this important word. We will then see that God's main purpose is not merely to make us happy in both this life and the next, but also to make us like Jesus Christ. This is sanctification in its fullest and deepest meaning.

There is a danger of oversimplifying the problem of man's fall. Adam's sin was followed by deep and wide implications both in the legal and moral realms; therefore, the raising of the hand, a decision for Christ, or a trip to the altar or inquiry room does not always solve the sin problem. Several things happened when Adam sinned: first of all, he died spiritually; second, he became guilty and subject to punishment, for, having broken the laws of God, he was a criminal; third, he became self-centered, choosing his own way instead of God's way, so that this selfishness became ingrained in his very nature; fourth, he became enslaved to a wily foe who had sought his fall and who now sought his eternal destruction.

Immediately after the sin and fall of Adam and Eve, God came to them and called them unto himself. His questions, "Where art thou?" and "What is this thou hast done?" were followed by the prophecy and promise of redemption: "I will put enmity between thee and the woman, and between thy seed and her seed: he shall bruise thy head, and thou shalt bruise his heel" (Gen. 3:15). The rest of the Bible is but a record of the unfolding, enlargement, and execution of this prophecy and promise.

The Fall made it necessary to bring into effect God's well-planned and perfect recovery program. This program includes calling sinners not only to repentance and faith in Christ but also, after the experience of justification and regeneration, calling those who have been saved to sanctification. The problem of the fall of man and sin is not solved by an experience of *imputed* righteousness. God will also *impart* righteousness if the conditions are met, for He *wants* to make us righteous; He *wants* to make us holy. Therefore, we ourselves must not be satisfied with any positional holiness, but need to be made holy. We need to be conformed to the image of Christ. "Him who knew no sin he made to be sin on our behalf; that we might become the righteousness of God in him" (II Cor. 5:21).

Each person of the Trinity, then, has a distinct and personal work to perform in our sanctification, and in this work of grace we must cooperate with the Father, with the Son, and with the Holy Spirit. The Father calls us to full surrender and entire consecration, and when this is complete, He gives us assurance of this experience. Far too many of us do not have assurance that we are wholly yielded to God. When a Christian is asked if he is wholly surrendered, the answer is often, "I hope so," or "I am surrendered as far as I know." But this experience of surrender is possible, and God expects it. When it is complete, He will bear witness to that fact, so we will know that it is complete. Such an initial surrender, however, will not preclude the necessity of obedience to further light. We must always bear in mind that surrender to God is not surrender into passivity, but rather a surrender unto obedience, so that we will give a quick and glad "yes" to *any* demand or request made by God along *any* line. Such an experience of surrender is the secret of prompt obedience and is absolutely essential.

We now want to consider in detail *sanctification through the Son*. The questions that come to us are these: "How are we sanctified through the Son?" "What does Christ do?" "What must we do?"

Read again Hebrews 13:11, 12: "The bodies of those beasts whose blood is brought into the holy place by the high priest as an offering for sin, are burned without the camp. Wherefore Jesus also, *that he might sanctify the people through his own blood,* suffered without the gate." This is a reference to the ritual on the Day of Atonement, an annual day of humiliation and expiation for the sins of the nation when the high priest made atonement for the sanctuary, for the priests, and for the people (see Lev. 16). It was celebrated on the tenth day of the seventh month by abstinence from ordinary labor, by holy convocation, and by fasting. It was the only fast enjoined by the Mosaic law, and hence was called *"the* fast" (Acts 27:9). First, the high priest, having put on his linen garments and entered with blood into the holy of holies, offered a sin-offering for himself and for the priesthood. He then took aside two he-goats for the nation—one he slew; and on the head of the other, the scapegoat, he laid the sins of the people, making it the sin-bearer of the nation. Then, typically laden with guilt, it was sent away into the wilderness. Presenting fully the work of Christ took two goats. The reason for this is that in its nature sin is two-fold. In the Bible we read of sins in the plural (acts of sin), and we read also of sin in the singular (sinfulness). It is worthy of notice that the Apostle Paul never mentions *sin* (singular) in the first chapters of Romans. From chapter 1 to 5:11 he speaks only of

33

sins (plural). But from chapter 5:12 to the end of the epistle he never mentions *sins* in the plural but only *sin* in the singular. It is also significant that in the first section of Romans in connection with *sins*, Paul speaks of the blood of Christ but never of the Cross. On the contrary, in the last section Paul never mentions the blood of Christ but only the cross of Christ. (The blood of Christ deals with *sins;* the Cross deals with *sinfulness.*)

The ritual of the Day of Atonement, then, carefully preserved this twofold nature of man's sin problem. There, in beautiful typology, we see in the slain goat Christ dying *for* our sins; and in the scapegoat we see Christ identifying himself with our sin and sinfulness, literally bearing it all away. Present-day theology rightly emphasizes the first aspect—that is, Christ *dying for* our sins. But we also need proper emphasis on the second aspect—Christ *taking away* our sins. Though we must never lose sight of the fact that "Christ died *for* our sins," yet we must also see that Christ, having identified himself with sinful humanity, suffered and died on Calvary's cross to *take away* our sins. In the language of the New Testament this double promise is set forth in the verses: "Behold, the Lamb of God, that *taketh away* the sin of the world!" (John 1:29); and "Now once at the end of the ages hath he been manifested to *put away* sin by the sacrifice of himself" (Heb. 9:26).

This double aspect of Christ's atonement is seen in many passages of Scripture. Consider Isaiah 1:18:

34

"Come now, and let us reason together, saith Jehovah: though your sins be as scarlet, they shall be as white as snow [first aspect]; though they be red like crimson, they shall be as wool [second aspect]." In this twofold promise, the first picture is of beautiful, white, falling snow. In Romans 4:7 David is quoted as saying, "Blessed are they whose iniquities are forgiven, and whose sins are covered." This is a picture of one aspect of our salvation—imputed righteousness. All looks pure under the covering of this snowy whiteness. But if God merely forgave the sins and left the sinner with a sinful heart and a sinful nature, it would be like covering him with pure white snow. That is not God's complete way of dealing with the sin problem. The prophet makes this plain in his words, "Though they be red like crimson, they shall be as wool." The thought there is not merely of imputed righteousness but of imparted righteousness, the making of every strand of our fallen, polluted, depraved nature pure and white as the white wool of the oriental mountain sheep—a wonderful and blessed possibility of grace! We must guard against the idea that God will conceal sin with a robe of righteousness. No! No! Nakedness is clothed, but not sin. Sin is *taken away*, and the righteousness of Christ is imparted to those who know the recovery power of the blood and the cross of Jesus Christ.

Also in Romans 5:10 this double aspect of Christ's atonement is seen: "If, while we were enemies, we were reconciled to God through the death of his Son [first aspect], much more, being reconciled, shall we be saved by his life [second aspect]." The most important experience for the sinner is to be reconciled to God; the most important experience for the believer is to be "saved by his life," to know the recovery power of the living Christ, who forgives and cleanses and delivers from the bondage of sin.

Finally, this twofold aspect is set forth in the first chapter of John's first epistle. Verse 7 states, "The blood of Jesus Christ his Son cleanseth us from *all* sin." In itself this is indeed a most wonderful and precious truth. However, verse 9 states another truth equally wonderful: "If we confess our sins, he is faithful and righteous to forgive us our sins, and to cleanse us from all unrighteousness." Verse 7 refers to *the blood* as the cleansing agent; verse 9 refers to *the living Christ* as the cleansing Agent. If verse 9 means anything at all, it means that Jesus himself personally undertakes to see we are cleansed and kept clean. Both verse 7 and 9 are all inclusive—*all* sin, *all* unrighteousness. The idea that sin must remain in every believer is erroneous and not based on Scripture. It is true that verse 8 does say, "If we say that we have no sin, we deceive ourselves, and the truth is not in us." This, of course, must refer to the one who will not put his faith in the blood and person of Jesus to cleanse him from sin and unrighteousness. It cannot possibly refer to one who has just been cleansed. If that were the case, John would be guilty of saying two directly opposite things. But this was not so. He was speaking of those who, either through ignorance or deception or indifference, are unwilling to come to Christ for this full and complete cleansing.

On Calvary's cross Jesus died for our sins. There He made full atonement. Now public justice is perfectly satisfied; now God is propitiated; we are reconciled to God; and we are redeemed by His blood. However, more than this legal aspect is involved in Christ's atonement. Our Redeemer took not only our sins to Calvary's cross, but there He took upon himself our very sinfulness. He, the Son of God, who had never sinned, identified himself with fallen man and took the sinful human race to the Cross. This is God's method of dealing with sin. As we have said already, let us repeat: sins *can* be forgiven; sinfulness of nature, however, can *not* be forgiven. The essence of sinfulness is selfishness, or selfness. Isaiah 53:6 says, "All we like sheep have gone astray; we have turned every one to his own way." This wanting to go our own way is unforgivable. God's only remedy is the Cross. This sin or selfishness must end in death—not physical death but in death to self. If one has any aspirations at all toward Christ-likeness, he must be willing to embrace the Cross in its fullest and deepest meaning and there die to sin, to self, to the world, and to the devil, and so be raised up a new creature in Christ Jesus. The disposition to have one's own way must be nailed to the Cross and Christ's way accepted. Self must be dethroned; Christ must be enthroned. This is a definite crisis experience.

Positionally, Christ took every member of the human race to Calvary's cross. This does not benefit one, however, until he accepts it as a fact and is willing to make all the necessary moral adjustments consistent with this fact. In other words, he must do exactly what Jesus said in Matthew 16:24, "If any man would come after me, *let him deny himself*, and take up his cross and follow me." To deny self simply means to give up all rights to one's self. Every sin that one ever commits can be traced back to some "right" reserved to one's self. A person has both legitimate and illegitimate rights, but a disciple of Jesus Christ must give up *all* rights. In the very nature of this problem we can easily see that forgiveness is not the full answer. Only identification with Christ in His death can solve this sin problem. It begins in a crisis experience of denying one's self, and continues by taking up the cross and bearing it every day. The crucified Christ must have crucified followers.

The Apostle Paul in Romans 6 makes the message of the Cross so very plain. In verse 6 he states the fact, "Knowing this, that our old man was crucified with him, that the body of sin might be *done away*, that so we should *no longer* be in bondage to sin." In verse 11 he tells us to count on this fact: "Even so reckon ye also yourselves to be dead unto sin, but alive unto God in Christ Jesus." This may involve certain moral adjustments, for one will be unable to reckon himself dead unto sin until he has died out to sin. For instance, the writer is now seated at his desk in his study. Would reckoning himself outside in the open air put him outside? No, not at all. He would have to make certain adjustments. He would have to leave his study and go outside. Then he could "reckon" himself in the open air. So also it is in the matter of being dead to sin—one must die to sin. The way to die to sin is to nail the disposition to have one's own way to the Cross; the way to reckon one's self alive to God is to enthrone Jesus Christ as Lord. In verse 13 of Romans 6, Paul gives us the practical outworking of knowing this fact of our crucifixion with Christ and counting on this crucifixion as a definite experience. He states that the life to follow is not automatic and therefore warns, "Neither present your members unto sin as instruments of unrighteousness; but present yourselves unto God, as alive from the dead, and your members as instruments of righteousness unto God." The best Scriptural summary of this experience is found in II Corinthians 5:14, 15: "The love of Christ constraineth us; because we thus judge, that one died for all, therefore all died; and he died for all, that they that live should *no longer* live unto themselves, but unto him who for their sakes died and rose again."

The psalmist David knew well the difference between sins committed and sinfulness, and he gives a very wonderful exposition of the subject in his penitential Psalm 51. He had sinned grievously, but in this psalm he indicates that he was stunned by the knowledge of his innate sinfulness. He first speaks of *transgressions*: "According to the multitude of thy tender mercies blot out my transgressions." After that, he brings his *iniquity* to God: "Wash me thoroughly from mine iniquity, and cleanse me from my sin." David sees that God wants more than legal cleansing, forgiveness, or pardon; and he says in verse 6, "Behold, *thou desirest truth in the inward parts;* and in the hidden part thou wilt make me to know wisdom." After stating the difference between sins and sin and that God wants to forgive and also to cleanse, David goes on to pray, *"Purify* me with hyssop, and I shall be clean: *wash* me, and I shall be whiter than snow." Then in verse 10 he adds, "Create in me *a clean heart*, O God; and renew a right spirit within me."

We can do no better than follow the leading of the psalmist David. After he had discovered he was guilty of sins committed and also that he was morally depraved, then he prayed along the line of what he had discovered. He confessed his sins and then cried out to God for heart cleansing; he prayed that he might have a clean heart and a right spirit. This should be our prayer. The place for the old life is the Cross. After making all necessary moral adjustments through a definite act of faith, one should reckon oneself dead to sin but alive to God. If this is done in faith, one can say with the Apostle Paul, "I have been crucified with Christ; and it is *no longer I* that live, but *Christ liveth in me*: and that life which I now live in the flesh I live in faith, the faith which is in the Son of God, who loved me, and gave himself up for me."

The second aspect of our sanctification, therefore, is the cleansing of the heart from indwelling sin through identification with Christ in His death and resurrection. In experience, all this becomes real when in faith one reckons oneself dead unto sin but alive unto God. Sanctification, then, means the dethronement of self, the enthronement of Christ, and a heart filled with perfect love.

CHAPTER FOUR

SANCTIFICATION
THROUGH GOD THE HOLY SPIRIT

FROM the Scriptures referred to, which attribute sanctification to each person of the Trinity, it seems to be conclusive that the Father, the Son, and the Holy Spirit each have a distinctive work to perform in the experience of our sanctification. We are sanctified by the Father; we are sanctified by the Son; we are sanctified by the Holy Spirit. We must therefore make a definite appropriation of the work of each person of the Trinity. Yet this should not be considered as three works of grace but rather as one great and important experience (also called the second blessing), which, to be complete, requires the work of each Person. This crisis experience is followed by growth in grace.

The Father's work in sanctification is to call one to full surrender and consecration to himself. When this surrender is complete, He will give witness that it is so. Concerning the Son's work, one is led to put faith in His blood and His cross to cleanse from all sin. Sins committed are forgiven and cleansed through the blood of Christ; however, sinfulness of nature can *not* be forgiven, for this is the spirit of selfishness, which is unforgivable. It must die. The Cross, not the blood, is the provision for this defect of nature. When one has nailed to Calvary's cross the disposition to have one's own will, then one can obey the command to reckon self dead to sin and alive to God. When this becomes real in experience, again there will be a witness that it is so. One may take deliverance from the power and depravity of sin just as definitely as one takes forgiveness. Later, through the Holy Spirit's work, there will be further cleansing, the cleansing and changing of traits and characteristics that may not be pleasing to Him, for the Holy Spirit will inspire us and enable us to bring about a character-likeness to Jesus Christ. (More will be said in Chapter 6 about this aspect of cleansing, which properly belongs to growth in grace following the crisis of sanctification.)

An excellent illustration of the threefold aspect of sanctification is provided in the erection and dedication of the tabernacle. First, the tabernacle, its furniture, and all its vessels were "set apart for God" in a ritual; second, they were sprinkled with blood; following that, the cloud covered the tent of meeting, and the glory of the Lord filled the tabernacle. So it is in the experience of a seeker after God. First, he must be *set apart* in full consecration; then he must be *cleansed* through the blood and the Cross. The result is that the glory of the Lord—the Holy Spirit—will come *upon* him to *fill* him.

Entire sanctification, properly experienced as a crisis subsequent to regeneration, is *one* act of grace. Yet for the purposes of discussion, it is helpful to consider different aspects, including the positive and negative sides which are as two halves of one sphere. The negative side is consecration and cleansing, and is preparatory. It is setting a vessel apart and cleansing it for a definite purpose—to be baptized and filled with the Holy Spirit. This latter is the positive side, and is the work of the Holy Spirit. Our present chapter, then, is concerned with the capstone—a very specific, instantaneous work of sanctification performed by the Holy Spirit. In the epistles of both the apostles Paul and Peter, sanctification is attributed to the Holy Spirit. Paul says, "We are bound to give thanks to God always for you, brethren beloved of the Lord, for that God chose you from the beginning unto salvation in sanctification of the Spirit and belief of the truth" (II Thess. 2:13). Peter writes, "According to the foreknowledge of God the Father, in sanctification of the Spirit. . ." (I Pet. 1:2).

Jesus prepared the disciples for both Calvary and Pentecost. Speaking of the Holy Spirit at that time, He said, "Whom the world cannot receive" (John 14:17). Old Testament typology (Leviticus 8 and 14) also carefully preserves this truth that the Spirit is not to come upon the world, nor upon flesh; for the anointing oil (a type of the Holy Spirit) was to be poured upon the blood (a type of Calvary). First came Calvary; then Pentecost. Moreover, in Exodus 30:32, the instructions for the holy anointing oil say, "Upon the *flesh* of man it shall *not* be poured. . . : it is holy, and it shall be holy unto you." (The prophet Joel's use of the word "flesh"—Joel 2:28, "I will pour out of my spirit upon all flesh"—indicates humanity and not moral quality.) Another beautiful picture in the Old Testament, Aaron's anointing (see Psalm 133), is no doubt a type of Christ's receiving the gift of the Holy Spirit and pouring it out upon the Church: ". . . the precious oil upon the head. . . ran down upon the beard, even Aaron's beard; . . . came down upon the skirt of his garments; like the dew of Hermon that cometh down upon the mountains of Zion." Christ received the gift of the Holy Spirit after His ascension and enthronement, and at Pentecost poured forth of the Spirit upon the Church: "Being by the right hand of God exalted, and having received of the Father the promise of the Holy Spirit, he [Christ] hath poured forth this, which ye see and hear" (Acts 2:33).

Every true Christian has the Holy Spirit in His regenerating capacity, for the Apostle says, "If any man hath not the Spirit of Christ, he is none of his" (Rom. 8:9); however, every Christian does not know Him in His sanctifying capacity. All are not baptized and filled with the Holy Spirit. We often hear the following explanation: "It is not that we receive more of the Spirit; it is only that He receives more of us. We cannot receive more or less of the Spirit since He is a person, and so either we have received Him

45

or we have not." But the fact is that if we cannot receive more or less of the Holy Spirit because He is a person, how can the Holy Spirit receive more or less of us since we too are persons? Yes, we *can* receive more of the Holy Spirit. We receive Him in regeneration to indwell us, and thereafter the more we yield to Him the more He indwells us, and the more He can control us. But His indwelling is not to be confused with the baptism with the Holy Spirit. There is a great difference between having the Spirit *resident* and having the Spirit *president*. The teaching that every Christian is baptized with the Spirit is one of the great deadening errors of the Church. Sometimes it has been said, "The Spirit was given to the Church, and therefore every true member of the Church, every true Christian, has received this gift, the baptism with the Spirit." But this is not so. Though Christ was God's gift to the world, yet to be saved one must receive Christ as Lord and Saviour. Even so, though the Holy Spirit is the gift to the Church, one must receive Him too in a definite experience in order to know victory in the life or power for service.

All true Christians have been baptized by the Holy Spirit into the body of Christ (I Cor. 12:13), but not all have been baptized *by Christ* with the Holy Spirit (John 1:33; Matt. 3:11; Acts 1:5). May the reader ponder these passages. Failure to see this important distinction is responsible for the lack of power in the Church today. Each person of the Trinity, though one in essence and in perfect unity, has certain delegated duties. One delegated duty of the Holy

Spirit is to baptize (to place) a penitent believer into the body of Christ; a delegated duty of Christ is to baptize a yielded, cleansed believer with the Holy Spirit. Jesus himself, as well as the apostles, was very definite on this point. The Holy Spirit is spoken of as "coming upon" and also as "filling" the believer, resulting in power for holy living and fruitful service. He imparts soul-saving power.

The early Church was a church of power because they did not confuse salvation and the baptism with the Spirit. Jesus made plain in His high priestly prayer that the disciples were believers (John 17). But He commanded these disciples to tarry in Jerusalem until they were clothed with power from on high. Likewise, a little later, the believers in Samaria were converted under the ministry of Philip; but they did not receive the Holy Spirit in the sense of the full blessing of Pentecost until Peter and John came down, prayed for them, and laid hands on them. Though Saul was converted on the Damascus road, it was not until three days later that he was filled with the Holy Spirit when he was ministered to by a little-known disciple named Ananias, who also laid hands on him. The Ephesian believers were called disciples (Acts 19:1), for they had been converted under the ministry of Apollos. Yet they had *not* received the Spirit; in fact, they did not even know that the Spirit had been given. Whether they were genuinely regenerated or not does not really matter, for Paul, accepting them as true believers, questioned whether or not they had received the Holy Spirit.

It was when Paul laid his hands on them that the Spirit came upon them, and they spoke with tongues and also prophesied (Acts 19:6). But from Acts 10 we learn that a long gap of time is not absolutely necessary, for Cornelius and his household, together with his friends, may have been saved and baptized with both the Holy Spirit and water on the very same day.

We see then from the Biblical record that being baptized with the Holy Spirit follows the experience of conversion and is not to be confused with regeneration. As we have said, the baptism with the Spirit is the capstone of our sanctification, for full consecration and cleansing are merely preparatory to this experience. Certainly the baptism with the Spirit is more than a blessed privilege; it is a definite necessity if one is to live on the level of Bible Christianity. No one is qualified to preach Jesus Christ until he is baptized with the Holy Spirit. Jesus sent no one out to preach Him until Pentecost. During Jesus' earthly ministry, after performing some notable miracle, He often said, "See thou tell no man." The disciples were authorized and sent to preach repentance, to preach that the kingdom of heaven was at hand, to tell what great things God had done for them. But to preach *Him*—to preach Jesus Christ himself—they were not qualified for that. It takes the Holy Spirit "sent down from heaven" to enable one to preach Christ rightly. Without the Holy Spirit they would preach a distorted, limited Christ. That is what the Apostle

Paul was afraid of when he said, "I fear, lest by any means, as the serpent beguiled Eve in his craftiness, your minds should be corrupted from the simplicity and purity that is towards Christ" (II Cor. 11:3). Then he goes on to mention the danger of preaching *"another* Jesus, . . . a *different* spirit, . . . a *different* gospel" (vs. 4).

This is exactly what is happening today. Instead of the Jesus of the New Testament, we have a distorted, limited Christ preached, a Christ who is able to get people only half saved. Instead of the Spirit and His power poured out at Pentecost, we are told that we are not to expect power now such as was known in the early Church, for that power was only for the apostolic times. Today the gospel has been tampered with, and more often than not, easy-believeism is presented as God's plan of salvation rather than the true gospel of regeneration and of salvation from sin and its power by the Holy Spirit. True conversion is *always* followed by a changed life. But today many conversions do not mark any change, nor do the converts show Biblical evidences of regeneration. The reason for this is that the gospel is not preached in the power of the "Holy Spirit sent down from heaven" but rather in the energy of the mind and of the flesh.

During this present age, the Father and Son do all things *in the Holy Spirit*. Apart from the Holy Spirit, individuals and organizations can accomplish nothing distinctly Christian. *He* is the strength of all that truly serve; *He* is the holy unction, power, and presence that makes a man a preacher, a true oracle of God; *He* is a teacher, advocate, and the only rightful authority in the Church. Thus in the early Church the disciples acted as the Spirit moved, decided as He prompted, and conformed to His program. But later, when the church usurped the authority of the Holy Spirit, it became an objective organization, dominated by human opinions, personal ambitions, and ecclesiastical decisions. This caused the loss of that once-known illumination, power, and inspiration. To perform the true functions of the Church today, all Christian organizations must again become instruments of the Holy Spirit.

However, without the baptism with the Holy Spirit, the Church will never rise to this exalted position of authority. Not only is this great truth untaught in the majority of churches, but also it is spoken against. Today the church's attitude towards the Holy Spirit is about the same as the attitude of religious leaders towards Christ in His day—that of rejection. Just as the priests of old were getting along very well by themselves and wanted no upset to their plans, so it is today. Church leaders are very satisfied with plans, objectives, and organization, and they want to keep things under control—that is, under their own control, not the control of the Holy Spirit. In William Law's writings, he refers over and over again to what he calls "the one thing needful—the immediate and continual inspiration of the Holy Spirit."

That there is much objection to this truth of the Baptism with the Holy Spirit, we are well aware. For instance, there is objection to using the term baptism for this experience. Though several other terms are in use, we prefer using the term baptism in order to distinguish it from the indwelling of the Holy Spirit. Thus the Holy Spirit *indwells* every Christian who has been genuinely regenerated, enabling him to live a victorious life; but the Holy Spirit *comes upon* or *baptizes* in order to give power and boldness for effective service. The *life* of a Christian begins at the Cross; his *service* begins at Pentecost.

There is no question that the Baptism with the Holy Spirit is also called the filling with the Holy Spirit. The reason for this is that the disciples at Pentecost were baptized and filled with the Spirit simultaneously. (Today, too, the baptism and the filling happen at the same time—even as justification and regeneration do.) Thus the experience may be referred to by either the term baptism or filling, the one always implying the other. However, it *is* right to call the initial experience the Baptism with the Spirit. This in Scripture is followed by *repeated fillings* for special needs. Peter, for instance, was "filled" in Acts 2:4 and also in Acts 4:31.

Concerning the term, the filling of the Spirit, we have often heard the objection, "It isn't that we receive more of the Spirit; it's that He receives more of us." To prove this point, some say, "The Holy Spirit is a Person, and since He is a Person, you receive Him—that is, all of Him. You cannot receive just part of Him since He is a definite Person; it is just a matter of His receiving more of us." Now at first this sounds good, but upon further consideration, we see that it is most illogical. If we cannot receive more or less of the Spirit because He is a Person, how then can the Holy Spirit receive more or less of us, for we are also persons? This argument therefore breaks down and is unworthy of consideration.

If we really want to receive the Baptism with the Holy Spirit, we must also get over another hurdle—namely, the teaching so prevalent today that the Baptism with the Holy Spirit is experienced *simultaneously with* regeneration. As we read the biographies of men who have been mightily used of God, we find that almost without exception they testify to having been filled with the Spirit *subsequent* to regeneration. (Though experiences of course are not the final criterion, five minutes of experience would correct much error in theology!)

There are several direct references to the Baptism with the Holy Spirit in the Scriptures. Each of the Gospels contains John the Baptist's statement regarding this experience. He contrasts it with his own baptism of repentance (Matt. 3:11; Mark 1:8; Luke 3:16; John 1:33). The term is also used by *Jesus Christ* himself in Acts 1:5: "John indeed baptized with water; but ye shall be baptized in [or with] the Holy Spirit not many days hence." *Peter* uses the expression in Acts 11:15–17 where he also describes it as "falling upon" and "the gift." The *Apostle Paul* uses the expression in I Corinthians 12:13: "In one Spirit were we all baptized into one body, whether Jews or Greeks, whether bond or free, and were all made to drink of one Spirit." Many writers and teachers build their whole doctrine of the filling of the Spirit upon this last reference. However, Paul had in mind an entirely different subject, for he was speaking of every believer having been quickened from the dead by the agency of the Holy Spirit and thus made a member of Christ's mystical body. This was the Pauline way of stating the new birth of John 3:7.

Let us now consider this experience of Jesus, of the disciples, and of today's believers. Jesus was *born* of the Spirit and all His life was *indwelt* by the Spirit, but until He was *baptized* with the Holy Spirit, He did not enter into His public ministry. Likewise the disciples. They were believers before Calvary, for Jesus had said they were not of this world and that their names were written in heaven (John 17:16; Luke 10:20); and although on the evening of that Resurrection Day Jesus breathed on them and said, "Receive ye the Holy Spirit" (John 20:20), yet not until fifty days later on the Feast of Pentecost did they experience the Baptism with the Holy Spirit. It was then that they were baptized and filled with the Holy Spirit for service (Acts 2:4).

53

And so it is today in the normal Christian experience. Every Christian is first born of the Spirit *and* indwelt by the Spirit, for "if any man hath not the Spirit of Christ, he is none of his" (Rom. 8:9). Certainly the more one yields to the Spirit, the more areas there will be for the Spirit to indwell. But, until the Baptism with the Spirit, this indwelling will never be complete. Thus, the indwelling of the Spirit *in* God's servant must not be confused with the Spirit *coming upon* God's servant to give boldness and power for service. It is this latter experience that is rightly called the Baptism with the Holy Spirit or, as some call it, the filling with the Holy Spirit, for He both clothes with power and fills at the same time.

Briefly, we must consider another objection that some raise against this wonderful experience. Some say that because the Holy Spirit was given to the Church at Pentecost, therefore every Christian already has this Pentecostal experience. When we compare this objection with John 3:16 where it says, "God so loved *the world*, that he gave his only begotten Son," then the objection breaks down. For in exactly the same way that Christ is God's gift to the world but everyone has not received Him, so the Holy Spirit is God's gift to the Church, but many in the Church have not received the gift of His Spirit offered them. In both cases there must be a definite personal appropriation.

Again we want to state clearly that we know every Christian *has* the Spirit. But at the same time, we also know that every Christian is not *filled* with the Spirit. There is an experience available for every Christian of being Spirit-filled, Spirit-controlled, and Spirit-empowered. And is not power the need of the hour? Today this is the universal cry from Christians, especially from those in full-time Christian service. We personally heard their cry, both in the homeland and in more than a score of other countries which we visited. "How can I receive power to serve the Lord effectively?" "I do not have the power I need." "I am so weak and do not have the power that the Bible offers." Everywhere it was made plain that *holiness* and *power* were the crying needs.

One of the familiar passages so frequently referred to concerning the receiving of the Holy Spirit is found in John 7. On the last day, the great day of the Feast of Tabernacles, Jesus had already drawn all eyes toward himself by His superabundant power and teaching. Then He made His great invitation: "If any man thirst, let him come unto me and drink. . . . But this spake he of the Spirit, which they that believed on him were to receive: for the Spirit was *not yet* given; because Jesus was not yet glorified" (John 7:37–39).

This last day of the feast, a Sabbath, was distinguished by very remarkable ceremonies. At a rather solemn moment, the priest brought forth water in golden vessels from the stream of Siloam, which flowed under the temple mountain, and poured it upon the altar. Then the joyousness of the feast broke out in loud jubilation as they sang the Hallel (Psalm 113–

118) and Isaiah 12:3: "With joy shall ye draw water out of the wells of salvation." This ceremony was commemorative of Moses' smiting the rock in Horeb, followed by the flowing of the historic stream of water, for "the Lord said unto Moses, Take thy rod, wherewith thou smotest the river, ... and smite the rock, and *there shall come water out of it* that the people may drink" (Ex. 17:5, 6). It was at this precise moment when all were thinking of the rock and the stream of water flowing from it that Jesus gave that great invitation, "If any man thirst, let him come unto me and drink."

That rock in Horeb was a type of Christ, for Paul said, "They drank of a spiritual rock that followed them, and the rock was Christ" (I Cor. 10:4). Thus the smitten rock in Horeb, from which the water gushed out, set forth the death of Jesus on the Cross under the stroke of divine judgment. But the water that flowed out was a type of the Holy Spirit, for the Bible never refers to water as a type of Christ, but rather refers to Christ as the giver of the water of the Holy Spirit. Thus, the flowing of the waters from the rock foreshadowed the outpouring of the living water of the Holy Spirit (which proceeded from Christ when He, the Rock, was smitten on Calvary). The water suggests the cleansing, refreshing, satisfying influences of the blessed Comforter. In John 7:38 Jesus said, "He that believeth on me, ... from within him shall flow rivers of living water"; then Scripture goes on to say, "for the Spirit was not yet given." Why was He not yet given? Because at the time at which Jesus was speaking,

Calvary had not yet come. Calvary in Scripture is closely associated with Pentecost, and the precious blood of the Lord Jesus with the Comforter. We cannot have the Holy Spirit apart from the Cross of Jesus Christ.

But how is the Baptism with the Holy Spirit received? God's Word says, "Received ye the Spirit by the works of the law, or *by the hearing of faith?*" (Gal. 3:2); and again, "He therefore that supplieth to you the Spirit, and worketh miracles among you, doeth he it by the works of the law, or *by the hearing of faith?*" (Gal. 3:5); "[Ye] receive the promise of the Spirit *through faith*" (Gal. 3:14). The way of receiving this blessing is not by works, nor by law, nor by excitement or noisy demonstration. The only way to receive the Baptism with the Spirit is *by faith*.

But why have so few received this gift? Because this gift is for the thirsty, and so few are thirsty. If one is living in sin, there is no thirst. Drinking of the world's cisterns never really satisfies and will take away the keen edge of the real thirst (that causes one to come to Christ for this great gift).

Another important fact that we need to understand is that it is Jesus Christ who gives this gift. From His own invitation in John 7 and also from the words of John the Baptist, we learn that Jesus Christ is the Baptizer. John the Baptist said to the multitudes, "I indeed baptize you in water unto repentance: but *he* that cometh after me . . . *shall baptize you* in the Holy

Spirit and in fire" (Matt. 3:11). Jesus himself stated that *He* is the One who gives the Holy Spirit: "If I go not away, the Comforter will not come unto you; but if I go, *I will send* him unto you" (John 16:7). Peter also definitely designated Jesus Christ as the One who poured out the Spirit in that wonderful experience, for he said on the day of Pentecost, "Being therefore by the right hand of God exalted, and having received of the Father the promise of the Holy Spirit, *he hath poured forth this*, which ye see and hear" (Acts 2:33). This verse clearly shows that after His exaltation, it was Jesus Christ himself who received this wonderful gift and who now pours it forth (gives it). Thus, from first to last, Jesus Christ remains the center of our Christian experience. This is very important and absolutely essential, lest one be led off from the truth of the centrality of Jesus Christ.

"If any man *thirst*, let him come unto me and *drink*," Jesus said. Thus Jesus compared this experience of receiving the Baptism with the Holy Spirit to a thirsty man drinking water. And how does one drink? Drinking is the easiest and most natural thing in the world for a person to do. One who is thirsty does not have to be taught *how* to drink, for he simply opens his mouth and takes in. Drinking is as easy as that. The application is clear. The Holy Spirit is a definite Person and though we cannot see Him, He is all around us. Like the air, He is here and at the same time in China and in Africa and in India. In receiving the Baptism with the Spirit, it may help to tell the Lord, "I know that the Spirit is here. I am thirsty for Him; I want Him. May He come upon me now. May He fill me now. Just as I breathe in this air, I receive Thy wonderful Holy Spirit."

An illustration may prove both interesting and helpful to those seeking the Lord.

When a friend of the writer was a little girl, she came one day into the living room and found their house guest, an elderly man, with his eyes closed and his hands cupped together. To her surprise, he was going through the motion of drinking out of his cupped hands. For a few moments she stood watching him, but at last, going over to him, she asked, "Whatever are you doing?"

"Oh," he replied, "I'm drinking of the Spirit. I'm so thirsty for God that I'm accepting Jesus' invitation, 'If any man thirst, let him come unto me and drink.' I'm drinking of the Spirit of Jesus, and He is filling me afresh with His own wonderful Holy Spirit."

This man was wonderfully used of God both in the U.S.A. and Britain. We too should drink of that wonderful stream, the Holy Spirit.

May every thirsty soul come to Jesus and ask Him for the Baptism and the filling with the Holy Spirit. Need we repeat that this blessing is only for those who have fully surrendered to God and who have been cleansed from all sin? Do what many others have done.

Make application to Jesus. Tell Him that you know He is the One to whom the gift is given; speak to the Rock; by faith ask and receive from Him the gift of the Holy Spirit. God will give assurance that this gift is now yours.

If one truly receives the Spirit by faith, he will receive the witness of the Spirit that it is so, for one knows when he has been baptized with the Spirit, and there is evidence of the Baptism with the Holy Spirit. For instance, if I am blind, I ask my friend concerning the landscape:

"Are there mountains?"

He answers, "Yes."

"Forests?"

"Yes."

"Flowers and trees?"

"Yes."

In my blindness I ask question after question and get what help I can. But when my eyes are opened or when the light of the morning breaks, *because I see it for myself*, I ask no more questions about the contour and the configuration of the landscape.

One infallible evidence is found in John 16:13, 14: "When he, the Spirit of truth, is come . . . he shall glorify me." The flesh cannot glorify Christ, nor can the devil. Only the indwelling Holy Ghost can truly glorify Him. When He has come upon us and filled us, He will glorify the Son.

Another evidence of this experience is the fruit of the Spirit: "love, joy, peace, longsuffering, kindness, goodness, faithfulness, meekness, self-control" (Gal. 5:22, 23). Now these are not nine fruits, but the description of one—love. These additional eight words give us quality, quantity, and flavors of the first fruit— love. If we have love, we have the other eight; if we lack love, we lack all.

Let me also say that one who has received the gift will have that inner knowledge which precludes the necessity for any further evidence that he is both *baptized and filled with the Holy Ghost* just as there is an inner knowing that one is *born* of God, *washed* in His blood, and *delivered* from the power of Satan and the self-life.

How, then, is one baptized with the Holy Spirit? *First of all,* he must know that this experience (sanctification, including the baptism with the Holy Spirit) is needed, and that it is available. *Secondly,* when one has been enlightened on this subject, he must seek in earnest. Three great hindrances to receiving this blessing are these: ignorance, fear, and indifference. All three must be met and overcome. Careful and prayerful reading of the Scriptures will give light to dispel the darkness of ignorance; fear must be recognized as not from God but from the enemy, and then be renounced and put away; indifference is "a Canaanite" hard to slay. And so one must be resolute, put away every weight, and begin to seek the Lord with the whole heart. At times one must take himself in hand and stir himself to seek that which God has promised.

Thirdly, there must also be a willingness to obey the Spirit in all things, for "the Holy Spirit is given to them that obey him" (Acts 5:32). Until this issue of willingness to obey is settled, one cannot hope to receive the gift of the Holy Spirit. The attitude of an unhesitating, joyful "yes" is essential.

Finally, one receives this blessing through faith. We read in Galatians 3:14, "That we might receive the promise of the Holy Spirit *by faith*." This wonderful gift and blessing, the Holy Spirit, was given to Christ at His ascension; now He gives Him to us. Thus to Christ himself we must come to receive this wonderful gift of the Holy Spirit—that is, be baptized and filled with the Spirit of God as were the disciples at Pentecost. This, then, is the capstone of our sanctification—the Holy Spirit producing character-likeness to Christ, and giving power for successful service.

CHAPTER FIVE

ISRAEL AN EXAMPLE

THE early history of Israel gives us a most wonderful picture of the salvation and sanctification experiences and also of the victorious life following the experience of entire sanctification. We are justified in this use of Israel as a type, for the Apostle Paul says that *"these things were our examples"* (I Cor. 10:6).

In the application of this typology to our experiences, let us begin with Israel in Egypt. In Exodus 1, Israel's condition was that of abject bondage. So helpless and hopeless was their situation that "Israel sighed by reason of the bondage, and they cried, and their cry came up unto God by reason of the bondage. And God heard their groaning and remembered his covenant with Abraham, with Isaac, and with Jacob. And God saw the children of Israel and took knowledge of them" (Ex. 2:23, 24, 25). At that time Israel's circumstances were indeed hard. Yet they had not begun that way, for at the very beginning of their sojourn, as guests of Egypt they were given the land of Goshen—the richest in all Egypt. There they became prosperous and multiplied. Israel was not in bondage to the Egyptians for years.

So also with bondage to sin. At first the devil does not reveal his hooks or his chains. No doubt special imps seek to enslave those who experiment with sin. Perhaps these nefarious characters say, "Do it again and you won't feel so bad about it." But "every one that committeth sin is the bondservant of sin" (John 8:34). Thus Israel in bondage in Egypt is a good type of a man today, who, experiencing Romans 7, cries out, "I am carnal, sold under sin. For that which I do I know not: for not what I would, that do I practise; but what I hate, that I do" (vs. 14, 15).

In Exodus 3 we read that God had compassion on Israel and sent His servant Moses to deliver them from bondage to Pharaoh. Then follows the record of God's ten plagues on Egypt, the last being the death of all the first-born. But from this judgment the nation Israel was saved through the application of blood on each doorpost at the time of the Passover Feast. What a wonderful story is Israel's salvation through the blood, followed by her deliverance in the Red Sea from the power of Pharaoh! Then the Israelites, free from Egypt and living in peace and hope, sang, "Sing ye to Jehovah, for he hath triumphed gloriously; the horse and his rider hath he thrown into the sea" (Ex. 15:21). For us, the crossing of the Red

Sea is a vivid picture of salvation from sin and from the power of the devil! A newborn Christian, like the Israelites, is generally full of joy and finds it easy to sing praises unto God.

But Israel's experiences did not end after they had crossed the Red Sea. Ahead was a conquest of the Canaanites, as well as a life to be lived in Canaan. For this they were wholly unprepared. Thus, though Canaan was directly northeast of the Red Sea crossing, God delayed their immediate entrance into the land and led them southeast by a way which in the Psalms is called "a straight way." (Geographically it was not a straight way, but it was straight for Israel because it was God's way.) First God led Israel to Mount Sinai where He purposed to give them the Law. To this Israel replied, "All the words which Jehovah hath spoken will we do" (Ex. 24:3). I am sure they meant it when they so confidently made that statement; however, they soon discovered that they had other commitments—commitments to the god, self. Of this, I suppose they were thoroughly unaware. Rejoicing in deliverance from the power of Pharaoh, they did not realize that they might still be in slavery—self-slavery.

The writer remembers a newly-born Christian who, when informed of the blessings of entire sanctification, looked upon him with pity and scorn as if to say, "Well, don't you know that I am saved?" Less than six months later this very person was found hanging by his own belt in a prison cell.

Just as Israel still needed deliverance after the Red Sea crisis, so it is today with souls who have been delivered from the world and the devil. Usually the self-life is not dealt with in the conversion experience of a seeking soul. At that time he is not capable of understanding his deepest needs. The Holy Spirit has brought conviction for sins committed and the need of a lost soul for a Saviour. This the sinner can understand. At the moment of conversion the Holy Spirit does not cloud the issue nor confuse the mind by bringing in the need of sanctification. Thus, while every genuinely converted person should thank God for the forgiveness of sins and assurance of eternal life, he should at the same time listen to the Holy Spirit as He, the faithful One, convicts of the need for sanctification. For sooner or later the saved one finds himself in the same position as Israel at Sinai— in need of deliverance from bondage to self. (Only when a need has become evident is there ever a seeking of deliverance from the self-life.)

This selfishness is something that can *not* be forgiven. As we said in Chapter 2, sins committed *can* be forgiven, but sinfulness of nature—that is, basic selfishness—can *not* be forgiven. It must die. Selfish acts can be forgiven; selfishness itself cannot be forgiven. It must end. The only provision for this problem is the Cross. The blood of Christ is God's provision for sins committed, but it is the Cross which provides the remedy for sinfulness of nature. In Paul's letter to the Romans, the first section, ending with 5:11, mentions sins in the plural only, never sin in the singular. This section refers to the blood but never to the Cross. From 5:12 to the end of Romans, sins in the plural are not mentioned nor is the blood mentioned, only sin in the singular and the Cross as God's remedy. This is certainly significant, and it refers to the twofold nature of sin and God's twofold means of solving the sin problem through the blood and the Cross.

Israel, as we have seen, had been delivered from Egypt (a type of the world) and from Pharaoh (a type of the devil) yet were in need of another deliverance. Full of self-confidence, they had to be convinced of the need for sanctification. Through the Law, God discovered to them the depths of their self-life, which had not been dealt with in their Passover and Red Sea crossing experiences. He gave the Law purposely to show them their great need for another work of grace. At the very border of the land of Canaan He revealed to them that they were thoroughly unready to enter. The Law had not accomplished its work, for it was intended to bring an end to their self-righteousness. But Israel had refused to die and was thoroughly unprepared and unable to enter the land at once. For their further discovery of this self-life, they were condemned to wander in the wilderness for thirty-eight additional years. (In the study and application of typology, one must consider the whole nation of Israel and not individual Israelites.) Then at the close of the forty years, they were again brought to the border of the land of Canaan—this time to the east side of the Jordan.

In the history of Israel there was a four-stage route to Canaan and victorious life and power. It began with *exhaustion*, for the forty years of aimless wilderness wanderings exhausted Israel. Furthermore, those years *exposed* to view Israel's need for a great moral change. Then on the eve of entering Canaan, Israel on the east side of the Jordan was ready for the third stage, *execution* in Jordan (type of death to self). Finally, they were *exalted* over the Canaanites in the land.

Even so with the believer today. He must come to a time when he is exhausted, self-exposed, and executed at the Cross, before he is exalted over his enemies. The Jordan is a type of the deeper meaning of Calvary—the Cross in the life of the believer. Jesus made the condition for discipleship plain: "Deny yourself, take up your cross and follow me." He laid the axe right at the root, not dealing with the perimeter of the problem but with the very center.

Every believer must be willing to give up all his rights, commit himself to Calvary's cross so that he can reckon himself dead to sin, allow the Holy Spirit to raise him up a new creature in Christ, and reckon himself alive to God. Only then is he ready to live in the land of Canaan, the land of victory. Just as the sinner, through his repentance and confession, puts the *blood* of Christ between himself and his past sins, so now does the seeking soul put the *Cross* of Christ between himself and his old life. This should be an experience just as definite as was the crossing of Jordan to Israel. The "old man" is put off altogether, for God's plan is not that one be a split personality—half old, half new—but rather that his "old man" be utterly crucified, dead, buried, and forever left in the grave. God's purpose is that we should be raised up new creatures in Christ Jesus—not only partly but wholly new. The Bible does not teach that we carry about with us an "old man" or a mine of corruption deep down in the depths of our being. It rather teaches that we are cleansed from all sin through faith in the blood and the cross of Jesus Christ. It teaches us to believe that we are new creatures in Christ Jesus and that we are to walk in newness of life.

At the Jordan River twelve tribal representatives were each commanded by God to take a stone from the east side of the Jordan, carry it into the river, and leave it there. Then these twelve representatives took up twelve new stones from the river's bed and carried them over to the west side of the Jordan and piled them up there for a memorial. This was God's way of saying that as stones from the wilderness side were buried in the Jordan and new stones carried out of the river, so also should Israel consider themselves both buried and raised a new nation. Such typology wonderfully illustrates the truth of Romans 6, where we are told that "our old man *was crucified* with him, that the body of sin might be done away, that so we should no longer be in bondage to sin" (Rom. 6:6). Next, we are exhorted to "even so reckon . . . also yourselves to be dead unto sin, but alive unto

God in Christ Jesus" (Rom. 6:11). Following this, the Apostle says that we are to yield wholly to God: "Present yourselves unto God, as *alive* from the dead, and your members as instruments of righteousness unto God" (Rom. 6:13). Israel was delivered from bondage to Egypt and to Pharaoh for a purpose. That purpose was to serve the living God. So also are we saved for a purpose. The Red Sea stands for the crisis of regeneration; the Jordan stands for the crisis of sanctification. Following these two experiences there is a life to be lived.

CHAPTER SIX

AFTER SANCTIFICATION, WHAT?

IN the land of Canaan God promised victory. To Joshua He said, "There shall not any man be able to stand before thee all the days of thy life: as I was with Moses, so I will be with thee; I will not fail thee nor forsake thee" (Joshua 1:5). Israel was given wonderful promises: "Every place whereon the sole of your foot shall tread shall be yours: from the wilderness, and Lebanon, from the river, the river Euphrates, even unto the hinder sea shall be your border" (Deut. 11:24). "He will deliver their kings into thy hand, and thou shalt make their name to perish from under heaven: there shall no man be able to stand before thee, until thou have destroyed them" (Deut. 7:24).

What are these but promises of the power of the Holy Spirit? It was only in the Spirit's power that Israel could destroy the Canaanites, possess the land, and dwell in it to fulfill God's purposes of blessing not only for Israel, but in turn for the entire world.

Such also is God's purpose for us Christians. We should not only be saved and sanctified and baptized with the Holy Spirit, but we should bless the entire world in the preaching of the gospel. We should make known the power of God to save from our enemies—from Satan, sin, self, and the world; yea, we should preach the transforming power of God that is able to conform us to the image of Jesus.

Israel was now in Canaan, a land possessed by hostile nations whose wickedness was so great that God commanded Israel to destroy them all utterly. So is it also in our Christian experience after the crisis of entire sanctification. Though in the land of victory, we are surrounded by enemies. First, then, *these Canaanites may stand typically for old habits* no longer becoming to the Christian. Such habits must be put off and put away. They perhaps suited the "old man" quite well, but they certainly do not fit the "new man," and so must be put off and put away altogether. Old habits of thinking, of working, and of eating must be put off. Abnormal appetites, passions, and desires must be brought back to normalcy. This does not happen at the crisis of sanctification, for God does not give us a new character. He gives us a new disposition, the disposition of Jesus, but we must make our own character. He gives us power to live right and to establish a proper Christian character. He shows us through the Word and by faith and obedience how we can be cleansed from traits and characteristics that are not pleasing to Him. These may not be sinful in the sense that they are things definitely called sin in Scripture, but they simply do not suit the "new man"; therefore they are to be put off and put away. The ever-blessed Holy Spirit will enable one to bring about a character-likeness to Jesus Christ. This is properly called growth in grace.

Many are looking for an experience that makes future faith and obedience unnecessary. But this is not God's way for us. We must walk in faith and possess the land. Israel was exhorted by Joshua to exploits of faith. Over and over again he said, "There is much land to be possessed." So also it is for us after the crisis of entire sanctification. We do not grow *into* grace but we grow *in* grace. Of course there is illumination and growth leading to the experience of justification. One, however, does not grow into it; justification is a crisis experience. Following justification, there is growth in the revelation of the need of entire sanctification; and one grows to the place where he sees not only that this is his need, but sees a work of God's grace provided for this need. Entire sanctification is a crisis experience. This, however, is followed by growth in grace. There is a life to be lived.

Secondly, *Canaanites may stand for evil spirits* who will contest our presence in the land. They harass and trouble many Christians, and must be destroyed. They can be bound and cast out. The Lord has condemned them to the lake of fire. These evil spirits attack in three different ways: The first we call *oppression*. This refers to evil spirits working in one's circumstances. They make life difficult for Christians. We cooperate with evil spirits by remaining ignorant of their devices. Their best secret weapon is the indifference of the saints. Their presence and working should be discerned. If they are recognized and in Jesus' name resisted, they must flee according to God's Word.

The second way in which evil spirits work we call *obsession*. In obsession evil spirits work primarily in the mind. In an advanced case of obsession, they control the thinking almost entirely. Many people are obsessed to some degree by fear and unbelief. They are in that measure obsessed by the enemy. Many are so obsessed that they remind the writer of a character whose stock saying was, "I ain't a going to like it." He had wholly sold out to negativism. Most people think in terms of inability, weakness, and even sickness and disease. This is the devil's work. He works through his evil spirits who plant weed seeds of doubt and fear in the mind. We must overcome the work of evil spirits in obsessing the mind by choosing to believe God instead of the enemy. In Jesus' name we ought to renounce definitely all ideas and suggestions received from evil spirits, and instead fill the mind with the truth of God. We should make positive affirmations along the statements of Scripture. These affirmations will generally be exactly opposite to the suggestions placed in the mind by the devil, for the enemy is negative; God is positive.

If one accepts oppression and obsession from evil spirits, the next stage is *possession*. Here the spirit gains control not only of the circumstances and of the mind but of the will itself. This person needs help outside of himself. Rarely is one who is possessed with evil spirits able to gain victory alone. We thank God that there are deliverers today who can set the captives free through the power of Christ. If, however, there is one possessed by evil spirits who does not have access to help, he can perhaps do no better than state audibly the ancient renunciation, "In Jesus' name I renounce the devil and all his works and all his ways; in Jesus' name I renounce every evil spirit; in Jesus' name I now take back all ground and every advantage I have given to the devil or any evil spirit. I now repent of my sins and surrender myself to Christ, and I trust Thee, Christ, to deliver me." If one goes this far, the Holy Spirit will lead further. If possible, help should be sought from one who is able to exercise the power of God to deliver.

To live the victorious life in the land of Canaan, one must have a good grasp of the objective truth of the gospel. He must know that Christ dealt with not only our sins but also our sinfulness. Thus he must know that Christ took not only our sins to Calvary's cross, but the sinner also. In God's mind and purpose, the sinner has been crucified with Christ, has died, and has been buried. The blessed possibility of being raised with Him is very true. Positionally, all Christians have been raised with Christ and are seated with Him in the heavenly places, as the Apostle so wonderfully states in his letter to the Ephesians.

This, however, must become real in experience. It becomes ours only when we believe what God has said. This faith, however, is impossible unless we have made all necessary adjustments. Full surrender and obedience are essential.

This, however, is but the crisis. It must be followed by a daily obedience. We must retain the spirit of Calvary. It is one thing to cross the Jordan, to commit self to the Cross; it is another thing to walk day by day in faith. Following the crisis of entire sanctification, the blessed possibility is of walking with a sure and certain tread and with absolute authority, holiness, and power, not only for a few moments or hours or days, but every day.

If one is to walk day by day in unbroken victory, he must not look for help within himself; rather, he must keep his eyes on the Lord. He must do as Joshua did. He was commanded to look to the Word of God. After the Lord gave him the wonderful promise that "there shall not any man be able to stand before thee all the days of thy life," he was told to meditate on the Word of God: "This book of thy law shall not depart out of thy mouth, but thou shalt meditate thereon day and night, that thou mayest observe to do according to all that is written therein: for then thou shalt make thy way prosperous, and then thou shalt have good success" (Joshua 1:8). So also we should look to the Word of God and meditate on it. We should look to the Lord—not to ourselves, not to our circumstances, but to Jesus Christ himself. And as we look to Him, He will give us all the power we need to live every day in victory and in fruitfulness.

CHAPTER SEVEN

POWER TO WITNESS

YE shall receive power, when the Holy Spirit is come upon you: and ye shall be my witnesses both in Jerusalem, and in all Judæa and Samaria, and unto the uttermost part of the earth" (Acts 1:8). The Lord Jesus Christ states categorically, "Ye shall be my witnesses." There are no if's or and's about it; *every* Christian is to be a witness—a witness of the saving power of God's grace. Along with this commission, however, is the promise of power, for no one can be a witness for Jesus Christ without the power of the Holy Spirit—at least no one can be an *effective* witness. I suppose there are sufficient witnesses, but many are witnesses without power, and most are witnesses without results. What an indictment! What a humiliation to be a witness for Christ with the promise of supernatural power, and yet to be fruitless!

Much modern evangelism is powerless, succeeding merely in producing those who profess to be saved but who lack Biblical evidence of regeneration. After a meager, unsatisfactory Christian experience, they are encouraged to believe themselves eternally saved from hell—though they are neither saved from sin nor from the power and dominion of the self-life. These so-called converts, though only "half-saved," are then urged to become witnesses, or soul-winners. The writer remembers in the early days of his own Christian life what great emphasis was placed on witnessing. Every one of us was told that he ought to be a soul-winner for Christ, and Acts 1:8 was cited to prove this point. However, not a word was said about the power of the Holy Spirit, who alone qualifies and enables one to be a true and effective witness to the saving power that is in Jesus Christ. As a result of our witnessing, no doubt a few were challenged and frightened enough to seek the kingdom. I suppose some stumbled in, but the net result of most of the witnessing then, as today, was very negligible. No successful businessman, contemplating the great number of members needed to produce the small number of converts, would consider the church a "going concern." Today our need is power.

Why, then, are orthodox fundamental believers so silent regarding the Holy Spirit and power? (Most messages and writings on this subject explain away the promise of power.) "An enemy hath done this." The devil has succeeded to a large extent in deceiving the Church into believing that all Christians have the Holy Spirit and power. The evidence, however, is entirely on the other side, for power is the scarcest commodity in the Church. Why should one deceive himself into believing he has that which is not evident in his life?

The record in the book of Acts definitely teaches that one can be saved and not be baptized with the Holy Spirit and power. For instance, the experience of the 120 disciples in the Upper Room, or of the Samaritans, or of the Apostle Paul, or of the Ephesian believers—all indicate that it is possible to be saved and yet not be baptized with the Holy Spirit. If Christ's words in His high priestly prayer mean anything at all, we must assume that the disciples were believers before Pentecost. Then on resurrection day, Jesus breathed on them, and they received the Holy Spirit. Before this time, Jesus had said that the world could not receive the Spirit; so the disciples were certainly saved souls on the eve of His resurrection. Likewise, the Samaritans were definitely saved souls before Peter and John came and laid their hands upon them, after which they received the Holy Spirit. The Apostle Paul no doubt was converted on the Damascus Road, but it was not until three days later that as a believing, committed, born-again Christian, the Holy Spirit came upon him through the ministry of Ananias. The only questionable incident is the case of Cornelius and his household. They may have been saved and baptized with the Holy Spirit the same day—though many Bible teachers believe that Cornelius was already regenerated when he called for Peter to come. But even if Cornelius was not a saved man when he called for Peter, the experience of justification and of sanctification and "enduement" of power would be separate works of God's grace. The time interval is unimportant. Finally, whether or not the Ephesian believers were evangelical Christians does not matter. The Apostle took them for such, and asked the question, "Did ye receive the Holy Spirit when ye believed?" (Acts 19:2).

The record of Acts is frequently explained away by saying, "*That* was but a period of transition; it is different today." Yes, it *is* different today. How different! How long must we remain different? We have a great number of believers without power. The Church will remain powerless as long as it receives its inspiration from man. We must look for inspiration from God. Fundamentalism speaks disparagingly of Roman Catholics because of their bondage to the Pope. But fundamentalists, too, have their own "popes," for each generation seems to produce at least one or more. (Rivals sometimes reign at the same time.) Their "encyclicals" are often as authoritative and binding as those of the pope at Rome. These popish writings sometimes appear in books or magazine articles. If a man attains to unusual stature, the encyclicals may appear as footnotes in the Bible. Multitudes recognize these footnotes as not inspired in the true Biblical sense, but accept them as authoritatively as the Scriptures. All such writings have one thing in common— the tendency to explain away the plain teaching of the Word of God regarding the baptism with the Holy Spirit and the subsequent power. This robs the ordinary believer—the trusting soul—of important parts of his Bible. Therefore believers must get back to the Word of God. We must search out not only the promises that are to be believed, accepted, and relied upon, but also the examples, the commands, and the warnings of the Scriptures.

At conversion one is supernaturally born of God. This experience of regeneration is always preceded by true repentance; it is always followed by the witness of the Holy Spirit. Before conversion, the sinner, condemned already, is on reprieve—a temporary delay in carrying out the sentence of the Judge of all the earth; following regeneration he begins that which can only rightly be called the period of probation. Thus conversion is not the end of the road but merely the end of the search for the right road. After this begins the pilgrim walk—the days of opportunity, privilege and power. Here obedience is essential. Though one is neither saved nor kept by obedience (any more than one is saved by repentance), it is, however, a necessary condition. Just as without true repentance it is impossible to believe God unto salvation, so also without obedience it is impossible to believe God for continuance in the Christian life. The reason is simple—one cannot walk at the same time in two directions.

Scripture states that the road, the right road, the highway of holiness, is safe: "A highway shall be there, and a way, and it shall be called the way of holiness; the unclean shall not pass over it; but it shall be for the redeemed: the wayfaring men, yea fools, shall not err therein. No lion shall be there, nor shall any ravenous beast go up thereon; they shall not be found there; but the redeemed shall walk there" (Isa. 35:8, 9). This road, however, has a ditch on either side. On one side is the ditch of Scripture mutilation, higher criticism, dead fundamentalism, "easy-believeism," dispensationalism; on the other side is the ditch of fanaticism, emotionalism, extremism, etc. One must keep on the way—the right way. The road is safe; the road is eternal. But we must keep on the road. This will qualify us for the receiving of power from on high. Power is not given as a reward for holiness, but it is given to those who are on the right way. The backslider, the disobedient, the unbelieving, do not qualify; the ignorant know neither what is promised nor how to receive; the deceived believe they have everything and are neither seekers nor receivers. (Their ministry is often "much ado about nothing," and after years of service they will look back to very unsatisfactory results.)

In conclusion, let us ask ourselves: Did Jesus promise the power of the Holy Spirit, or did He not? Did He promise that the works that He did we should do also, and greater works should we do? Yes, these are promises of our Lord Jesus Christ himself, for He said that this power should be ours because "I go unto the Father." When He went unto the Father, He sent the wonderful Holy Spirit of power to come *upon* (not only to dwell *within*) every seeking, prepared soul. The question we must answer, then, is this: "Do I have this power?" If my answer is no, then there is another question: "Am I willing to make every necessary adjustment so that I can seek and receive this power?"

CHAPTER EIGHT

A GUIDE TO SEEKERS*

IF we are to seek and find God, if we are really in earnest about seeking a satisfactory experience and relationship with Jesus Christ, a few words of instruction are in order. This is the time to be definite and specific. It is not the time to pray for any other thing but for the one thing needful—a right relationship with Jesus Christ and power to serve Him effectively. Too often in an after-meeting those seeking God pray for everything except that one thing needful. Though awakened, convicted, and convinced, seekers may still need guidance in their seeking and finding a satisfactory Christian experience, and for this reason we feel led to give these simple instructions. Of course they are not intended to be a substitute for the Holy Spirit; rather, their purpose is to center the thoughts on three main issues, so that the Holy Spirit may lead in making definite commitments along definite lines.

The first thing is to consider and settle the problem of sin. Sin is a barrier, and as long as it remains in the

*This chapter was written originally as a tract and is available in tract form at Bethany Book Shop, 6820 Auto Club Road, Minneapolis 20, Minn.

soul, it will separate from God. We must be absolutely honest with God. The sinner's prayer, "God be merciful to me a sinner," is always in order. Besides this, we must confess every sin that the Holy Spirit has brought to our attention. Each must be repented of; it must be confessed; it must be abandoned. Repentance means a change of mind, a turning about. We must turn from all sin with the intention of having nothing more to do with these things of which the Holy Spirit has convicted us. Each must be confessed and put away.

After being absolutely honest with God, we must believe His Word and trust Him to forgive and cleanse. His Word is very specific on this point and says, "If *we* confess our sins, *he* is faithful and just to forgive us our sins, and to cleanse us from all unrighteousness" (I John 1:9). We must *trust the Lord* to wash these sins away in Jesus' blood. Confession alone is not enough; we must also receive forgiveness. God is willing to forgive every penitent soul, and He *will* forgive for Jesus' sake. Yet this forgiveness must be received, and is ours when we receive it.

But we must be thorough, for this is no time for haste. The peace that is sure to follow, as well as the depth of our Christian experience, will be exactly commensurate with the thoroughness with which we deal with the sin problem. Sin may have gone deep down into the soul; but even so, the blood of Jesus can go deeper still and *will* cleanse, for the Word says, "The blood of Jesus his Son cleanseth us from *all* sin"

(I John 1:7). When this truth is known, accepted, believed, and received, peace will be the result. This is the peace of forgiveness. This is the first step.

But you may say, "I *have* confessed my sins to God, and I still don't have peace. I don't seem to be able to receive the assurance that my sins are forgiven." There may be the need for restitution. Stolen things must be returned; harsh words, unkind acts toward others *may* have to be confessed directly to others, as well as to God; things said that were not true will have to be straightened out. Restitution is important and essential. Some earnest but misguided people believe that restitution is unnecessary. They say that every sin can be washed away in Jesus' blood, and that it is not necessary to confess to the person sinned against. But this is not correct, and could be the reason that the world has so little respect for Christians. The world expects us to straighten out our lives if we have become Christians. The world expects us to straighten out even the past. Now we all know some sins cannot be straightened out and are better left untouched. God himself will take care of these things. But everything that *can* be straightened out should be corrected. The general rule is that confession of sin should involve as many persons as the sin involved. If the sin was against God alone, then confession to God alone is sufficient. If the sin was against God and another person, the confession should be to both. If the sin was against God and a group of people, it should be confessed to God and that group. Sins of immorality should never be confessed to a group and perhaps should never be confessed to another person. It is better that they be confessed to God alone and left there. He in His mercy will forgive and cleanse and enable the person to live a pure life in the future. Sins of attitudes or criticisms usually need to be confessed to God only. But we should be thorough in this matter of dealing with sin. If we are willing in our hearts to make every restitution indicated, God knows it and will lead in this important matter. He will give peace and joy in making whatever restitution the Holy Spirit deems necessary. This also will eliminate the possibility of our own conscience accusing us in the future.

We are not suggesting endless introspection. This business of searching for sin is the Holy Spirit's work, and not ours. We are to confess, to abandon, to correct those things that the Holy Spirit brings to our attention. He is faithful. He is thorough. He can be trusted. The enemy of our souls would like to call attention to things that have been forgiven and straightened out long ago. If the sin *has* been confessed, if restitution *has* been made, if forgiveness *has* been received, then that sin is gone *forever* and should never trouble us again. The enemy of our souls may want to bring to our attention past sins that have been forgiven. But he should be ignored and resisted, for the Bible says if we resist him, he will flee (James 4:7). We thank God for His perfect remedy for sin.

The second step in seeking God is to surrender wholly to God. Even though past sins are thoroughly dealt with, unless a person will surrender wholly to God, they will reoccur. No partial surrender will do. It must be complete; it must be irrevocable. This surrender must be so complete, so total, so unalterable, that the only word that can properly describe it is death—death to self. Past sins may have been thoroughly taken care of; they may have been confessed and washed away in Jesus' blood. But they will reoccur unless a person comes into the experience of full surrender to God. Only the surrendered soul can be led by the Spirit of God. The one who is not fully surrendered may be led at times, but the only safe walk for a Christian is that of full surrender and complete obedience to the will of God *in everything*.

To clarify the matter of surrender, let us insert a word here. If one has never initially received Jesus Christ as Lord and Saviour, these two steps of confession of all sin and of total surrender are preparatory to this experience of inviting Jesus Christ to come into the heart and take His rightful place as Lord. The Word of God says that "as many as received him, to them gave he the right to become the children of God" (John 1:12). Only the person who has confessed sin and trusted God to forgive him for Jesus' sake is ready to receive Jesus as Lord and Saviour. Such a one will be born again and become a new creature in Christ Jesus. This is a definite crisis experience.

But someone may already have assurance of sins forgiven and assurance of eternal life, but may not be satisfied with his present Christian experience.

Such a one needs to make sure that he is fully surrendered to God in everything. A ship tied to the shore with several cables is not free until the last cable is loosed. So also in the matter of surrender. Many things may have been given up, but a person is not surrendered until the *last* thing which holds back is utterly given up. This surrender should be so thorough, so irrevocable, that it will never have to be repeated.

In a sense, of course, it may be called an "open" surrender in that it would include everything and anything *in the future*. But at the same time, it must be so complete that both the person and God know that this issue is settled. It is like signing a blank check and giving God permission to fill in any amount that would please Him both at the present and future. It is like signing a contract and letting God fill in all the provisions and the conditions. God knows when this is complete and He will witness to it. So often we hear someone say, "I am surrendered *as far as I know*." That is not far enough. When one is surrendered fully, he knows it. He knows it because his own heart witnesses to it. Besides, the Holy Spirit will witness that it is complete. If one is seeking that satisfactory Christian experience, that relationship with Christ that the heart really longs for, if one is seeking power from on high, he must not only have dealt with all sin, but also he must have surrendered *wholly* to God.

Scripture gives further light on all this in Romans 6:1–14. When Christ died, He took not only all *our sins* to the Cross, but He also gathered up the whole sinful race and bore us all to Calvary (II Cor. 5:14, 15). In the mind and the purpose of God, the whole Adam race died when Christ died. While this is true of everyone, it does not benefit us until we make this total surrender. It is exactly the same as it was with our sins in the initial experience with God. Two thousand years ago Jesus certainly took all our sins to the Cross: "Who his own self bare our sins in his body upon the tree, that we, having died unto sins, might live unto righteousness" (I Pet. 2:24). The Word also says that "he is the propitiation for our sins; and not for *ours* only, but also for *the whole world*" (I John 2:2). This, however, did not benefit us individually until we knew it, until we believed it, until we accepted it. It was then that we were actually forgiven of our sins. It is exactly the same regarding this deeper truth. Christ took us all to the Cross, and there when He died, we died; when He was buried, we were buried; when He rose again from the dead, we rose again from the dead; when He ascended, we ascended; when He was seated on the right hand of God, we were seated with Him. But this does *not* benefit us until we see it, know it, believe it, and accept it. It does not benefit us until by faith we *reckon* ourselves dead to sin and alive to God (Rom. 6:11). But this we cannot do without making a full surrender to God.

The initial step of salvation means that a person is converted from self to God. The full implication of this, however, does not always dawn on us at first. It is afterwards that we discover the need of this *total surrender*. Now it is a fact that Christ took us to Calvary's cross. Yet there are several moral adjustments that need to be made *before* we can reckon on this great truth in such a way that we have assurance that it is so. That which is positional for all must become a reality. The first moral adjustment, of course, is to be honest with God regarding sins, and then to put our faith in Jesus' blood to wash them away. The second moral adjustment is in the matter of surrender. If we have dealt with sin and surrendered wholly to God, we will find ourselves *able* to reckon ourselves "dead to sin but alive to God." This brings deliverance from the bondage of sin. "Knowing this, that our old man *was* crucified with him, that the body of sin might be done away, that so we should no longer be in bondage to sin" (Rom. 6:6). "Reckon ye also yourselves to be dead unto sin but alive unto God in Christ Jesus" (Rom. 6:11).

Now we know that every good thing is "in Christ." But we receive in stages. It appears that we are not able to take everything at once; therefore, after the crisis of salvation, God discovers to us deeper needs, and it is then that He shows us all that is implied in receiving Jesus Christ as Lord. We praise God for the possibility of coming into that right relationship with the lordship of Christ. (Lordship is essential to salvation, but the full implications are not understood at the time of salvation.)

The third step in seeking God is to ask for and receive the gift of the Holy Spirit. The first two steps of forgiveness and surrender are but preparatory. One must also be "clothed with power from on high." One must be "filled with the Holy Spirit." Every Christian *has* the Holy Spirit, but every Christian is not *filled* with the Holy Spirit. The disciples were children of God before Calvary. On resurrection day, Jesus breathed on them and said, "Receive ye the Holy Spirit." They received the Holy Spirit then but were not filled with the Spirit. On the same day He also said, "I send forth the promise of my Father upon you: but tarry ye in the city, until ye be clothed with power from on high" (Luke 24:49). This "clothing with power" did not happen on that day but at Pentecost fifty days later. So also with Christians today. It is possible to be born of God, to have the Holy Spirit indwelling, and still not be "clothed with power from on high" or "filled with the Holy Spirit." Yet if one is cleansed from all sin and wholly surrendered to God, he is a proper candidate for this wonderful blessing and experience. At Pentecost the disciples were both clothed with power from on high and also filled with the Holy Spirit (Acts 2:1-4). This experience must be received by faith.

Christ is God's gift to the world; the Holy Spirit is His gift to the Church. We all understand that though Christ is God's gift to the world, still He has to be individually appropriated. So also regarding the Holy Spirit, for He is the gift to the Church, but must be individually appropriated. The wonderful gift of the Holy Spirit has been given to Christ, and it is He who gives the Spirit to us. John the Baptist made this very plain, explaining that though he himself baptized with water, One would come who would baptize with the Holy Spirit and fire (Matt. 3:11). Jesus himself also claimed the giving of the Spirit to be His special prerogative. More than once He said, "I will send him unto you" (John 16:7, 8). On Pentecost Day, Peter, too, explained this, for we read in Acts 2:33, "Being therefore by the right hand of God exalted, and having received of the Father the promise of the Holy Spirit, *he hath poured forth this*, which ye see and hear."

Therefore, to receive this wonderful gift, this wonderful blessing, the baptism and filling with the Holy Spirit, we are to come directly to Christ himself. He gave us an invitation saying, "If any man thirst, let him come *unto me* and drink. He that believeth on me, as the scripture hath said, from within him shall flow rivers of living water. *But this spake he of the Spirit*, which they that believed on him were to receive: for the Spirit was not yet given; because Jesus was not yet glorified" (John 7:37–39). Jesus spoke these words at a significant time, for it was when the Jews were commemorating the rock smitten by Moses' rod at Horeb. In the mind's eye of all Jesus' listeners was a great rock, and from that rock gushed forth a great stream of water. The Apostle Paul made plain to us that this rock typified Christ; in fact, Paul actually said, "That rock was Christ" (I Cor. 10:4).

The water gushing from the rock is a type of the Holy Spirit. The Apostle John well knew the meaning of this, for he said, "This spake he of the Spirit." We are to come to Christ and drink of the Spirit, for He will both baptize with the Spirit and He will fill with the Spirit. It is the Lord Jesus Christ who gives this wonderful Gift.

But *we must come to Him and receive* by faith the Gift which He offers. There is proceeding from Him now that great stream not of water but of Spirit, and anyone who will come to Him in faith will be clothed with the power of the Spirit. He will be filled with the Spirit.

Yet to receive this wonderful blessing we must be clean, we must be empty, we must be low. If one has met the conditions for forgiveness, if one has surrendered wholly to God, then he *is* clean, he *is* empty. If we will come humbly to the Lord in faith and obedience, we will be proper candidates for this great gift—the gift of the Holy Spirit. He is given to those who obey Him (Acts 5:32). He is given to the humble.

These three things then are essential: *first,* a proper dealing with the problem of sin, as well as faith to receive forgiveness and cleansing; *second,* full surrender, as well as faith to believe that God has received what has been given to Him; *third,* the gift of the Holy Spirit to be received by faith from Christ, for it is He who gives this wonderful blessing. Note that this gift is to come "upon" us, that is, to clothe us with power from on high, and also to come "within" us to fill the life. We need to be *filled* with the Holy Spirit to give us power to live a holy life; we need Him *upon* us, to be clothed with Him, to receive power for service. Such is God's wonderful provision to be received by faith.